# Amazing Ancient Cultures of the World

# About Wise & Wide

- A systematic 6-level English reading program based on Lexile® measures
- Diverse and interesting topics chosen from the elementary curriculums of Korea and English speaking western countries
- Well-written books in various forms including fiction stories, descriptive texts, and classics retold
- The informative but original fiction stories grab your interest, leading to the easy and clear understanding of the educational content.
- Improve thinking skills with solid after-reading activities at all levels of the series.

**Wise & Wide** is a 6-level English reading program that consists of 60 books and each level is systematically divided by Lexile® measures. The Lexile® Framework for Reading is the most popular reading measuring system in American formal education curriculums and many English programs. Over 20 out of 50 states in the U.S. mark Lexile® measures directly on students' final report cards and over 300 well-known publishers adopt and use Lexile® measures.

Experience many kinds of readings written by professional writers from the U.S. and England. They used interesting topics that were carefully chosen after analyzing elementary curriculums from around the world including Korea, the U.S., England, and Australia among many others. Comprehensive after-reading activities including graphic organizers, speaking tasks, and After-reading Tests are ready for you.

## Levels in the series and their corresponding Lexile® measures

| Level | Lexile® measures | U.S. Grade |
|-------|------------------|------------|
| Level 1 | Below 200L | Pre K - K |
| Level 2 | 190L - 400L | Lower Grade 1 |
| Level 3 | 350L - 530L | Upper Grade 1 |
| Level 4 | 420L - 650L | Grade 2 |
| Level 5 | 520L - 940L | Grade 3 - 4 |
| Level 6 | 830L - 1070L | Grade 5 - 6 |

＊ Smart Readers: Wise & Wide level 1 is applicable to the preschool level in the U.S.

＊ The source of the relationship between Lexile® measures and U.S. school grades: CCSS(Common Core State Standards) FOR ENGLISH LANGUAGE ARTS, APPENDIX A (2012, which is used by 45 states in the U.S.)

# Topic List

| | Level 1 | Level 2 | Level 3 | Level 4 | Level 5 | Level 6 |
|---|---|---|---|---|---|---|
| **Book 1** | Science>Biology: The hibernation of animals Story | Science>Biology: Living and nonliving things Story | Science>Biology> Animals & the Environment: Sea otters Story | Environment> Living with nature: The diver & the persimmon tree Story | Science>Biology> Animal: Amazing animals of the Amazon Story | Science>Biology: Germs, transmitted diseases Story |
| **Book 2** | Literature> World classics: Aesop's fables Story | Literature> Traditional fairy tale: Old tales about stones Story | Social Studies> Economy: To run a business to make and save money Story | Science>Biology> Plants: Photosynthesis Story | Science>Earth science: Earth's layers, earthquakes, volcanoes, and earth's atmosphere Report | Mathematics> Sequence: The golden ratio & the Fibonacci sequence Story |
| **Book 3** | Science>Physics: How shadows are formed Story | Literature> World classics: Peter Pan Story | Science>Scientific technology: Nanobots Story | Literature>Myths: World's creation stories Story | Literature> Legend: The story of King Arthur Story | Literature>Myths: Constellation myths Story |
| **Book 4** | Literature> Traditional literature: The Talmud Story | Science>Biology> Animal: Polar bears Story | Science>Biology> Animal: Mountain gorillas Story | Social Studies> Cultural anthropology: Amazing ancient cultures of the world Story | Science> Earth science: Clouds and weather Story | |
| **Book 5** | Social Studies> Ethics: Rules in daily life Story | Science>Biology : The five senses Report | Social Studies> Cultural anthropology: Astonishing festivals Report | Art>Music: Stories from two operas Story | Social Studies> World culture & history: The Renaissance Story | |
| **Book 6** | Social Studies> World geography & travel: Tourist attractions around the world Story | Science>Biology> Animal: Dinosaurs Story | Science> Astronomy: The solar system Story | Social Studies> People: Three great people who overcame hardships Story | Science>Scientific technology: The wonderful world of robots Report | |
| **Book 7** | | | | Science & Social Studies> Technology & culture: Inventions from around the world Report | Art>Works of art: Famous paintings Report | |
| **Book 8** | | | | | | |
| **Book 9** | | | | | | |
| **Book 10** | | | | | | |

* 10 books in each level will be published.

# How to Use
# This Book

## •Before Reading

You can easily find the topic and what kind of story you are about to read.

### Before Reading

## Amazing Ancient Cultures of the World

Level 4~4,
Lexile®630L

**Special mission! Protect unique global culture!**

Preserving various ancient cultures is something that we must do for future generations. As part of this effort, a specialized agency of the United Nations, UNESCO evaluates various cultural heritages around the world according to their historical, scientific and artistic value, etc., and it designates them as world heritages. Such world heritages designated by UNESCO get various types of heritages. World heritages designated by UNESCO include ancient Maya cities, Viking remains, etc.

In the book, you will meet fictional characters who represent Central and South American, European, Oceanian, and Middle Eastern cultures among the various ancient cultures around the world and you will learn about their ancient cultures.

The reason why current mankind has each country and ethnic group's unique characteristics of culture and leads their own lives is that they have their own culture that each ethnic group's ancestors had preserved.

### Summary

One day, Chac and Neli, two Maya boys who loved exploring the jungle, looked around a Maya pyramid, an observatory, etc., and talked about the unique culture of the Maya.

A Viking girl in Europe, Helga helps her mom like other Viking girls and does various household chores. Through Helga's family who prepare a variety of foods for a festival and get ready to go to war, you can get a glimpse of Viking culture.

Natives of New Zealand, Rongo and Aata, two Maori boys, practice Maori traditional dances with joy. Rongo tells his friend, Aata a story about tattoos that show different characteristics of the Maori people along with their traditional dances.

Finally, you will meet Noora's family, Bedouins who travel around deserts. One day, someone visited Noora's family tent. How do Noora's family who have a tradition to treat their guest with heartwarming hospitality greet the guest?

## •The text

All the stories were written by professional writers from the U.S. and England, so you will read authentic and appropriate English sentences and expressions in every book in the series.

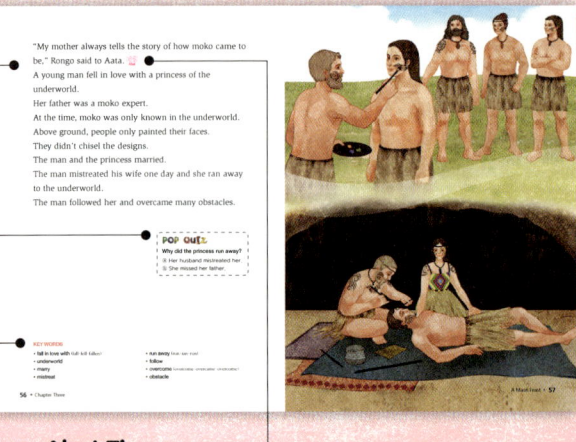

"My mother always tells the story of how moko came to be," Rongo said to Aata.
A young man fell in love with a princess of the underworld.
Her father was a moko expert.
At the time, moko was only known in the underworld.
Above ground, people only painted their faces.
They didn't chisel the designs.
The man and the princess married.
The man mistreated his wife one day and she ran away to the underworld.
The man followed her and overcame many obstacles.

**POP QUIZ**
Why did the princess run away?
ⓐ Her husband mistreated her.
ⓑ She missed her father.

**KEY WORDS**
• fall in love with 사랑에 빠지다
• underworld
• marry
• mistreat

• run away 달아나다, 도망치다
• follow
• overcome 극복하다, 이겨내다
• obstacle

56 · Chapter Three                                      A Maori boot · 57

## •Pop Quiz

Check out right away if you understand what you have just read by solving a pop quiz that checks your comprehension.

## •Key Words

The key words and expressions on each page are listed for you to easily study them.

## •Aha! Tips

Download free Korean explanations at *www.ihappyhouse.co.kr* for all of the sentences marked with "Aha!". These explain cultural, scientific, and economic knowledge or they deal with aspects of English such as grammatical structures or idiomatic expressions. There are lots of "Aha! Tips" to help you understand the text.

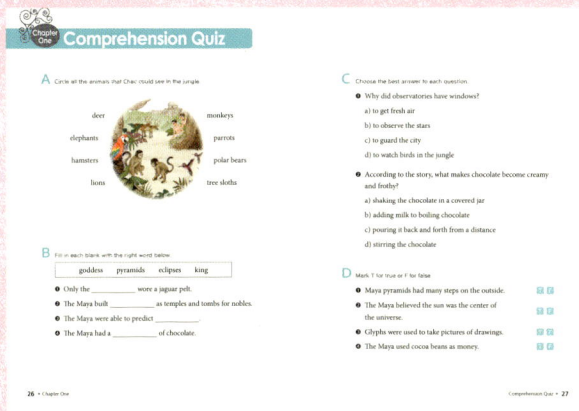

## •Comprehension Quiz

After reading one chapter, solve various questions to find out if you fully understand the content.

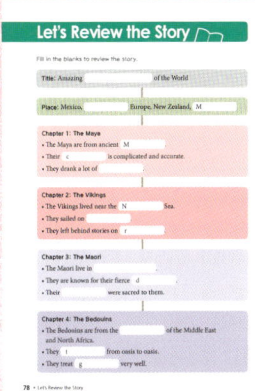

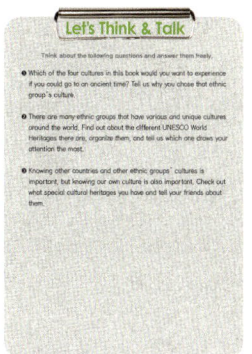

## •Let's Review the Story /
## •Let's Think & Talk

Fill in the blanks in the organizer to summarize the whole story. Express your own thinking and feelings about the story by answering the questions. You can build up logic and reasoning skills for your essay examinations in the future.

## Appendix

### Audio CD
In the CD audio book form, the texts are read vividly by American professional voice actors.

### After-reading Test
Solve an additionally provided After-reading Test for each book.

### The Korean translation, Answer Keys, a Word Quiz, a Word List, and Aha! Tips for each book
You can download them for free at *www.ihappyhouse.co.kr*

# Before Reading

## Amazing Ancient Cultures of the World

Level 4-4,
Lexile®630L

•Social Studies〉Cultural anthropology
•Story

### Special mission! Protect unique global culture!

The reason why current mankind has each country and ethnic group's unique characteristics of culture and leads their own lives is that they have their own culture that each ethnic group's ancestors had preserved.

Preserving various ancient cultures is something that we must do for future generations. As part of this effort, a specialized agency of the United Nations, UNESCO evaluates various cultural heritages around the world according to their historical, scientific and artistic value, etc., and it designates them as world heritages. Such world heritages designated by UNESCO get various types of protection. World heritages designated by UNESCO include ancient Maya cities, Viking remains, etc.

In the book, you will meet fictional characters who represent Central and South American, European, Oceanian, and Middle Eastern cultures among the various ancient cultures around the world and you will learn about their ancient cultures.

## Summary

One day, Chac and Nelli, two Maya boys who loved exploring the jungle, looked around a Maya pyramid, an observatory, etc., and talked about the unique culture of the Maya.

A Viking girl in Europe, Helga helps her mom like other Viking girls and does various household chores. Through Helga's family who prepare a variety of foods for a festival and get ready to go to war, you can get a glimpse of Viking culture.

Natives of New Zealand, Rongo and Aata, two Maori boys, practice Maori traditional dances with joy. Rongo tells his friend, Aata a story about tattoos that show different characteristics of the Maori people along with their traditional dances.

Finally, you will meet Noora's family, Bedouins who travel around deserts. One day, someone visited Noora's family tent. How do Noora's family who have a tradition to treat their guest with heartwarming hospitality greet the guest?

# Contents

# Amazing Ancient Cultures of the World

# Amazing Ancient Cultures of the World

# Ancient Cultures

Every culture, no matter the time or place, has something to teach us.

Once upon a time, the Maya people lived in the jungles of Central America.

Between 1500 BC and 900 AD, the Maya built amazing structures, watched the stars, and drank chocolate. 📖 Aha!

After the Spanish discovered Central America, they brought chocolate back to Europe.

Now the whole world enjoys chocolate.

**KEY WORDS**

- ancient
- culture
- no matter
- once upon a time
- Maya
- Central America
- between A and B

- BC (*cf.* AD)
- build (build-built-built)
- structure
- drink (drink-drank-drunk)
- the Spanish
- discover
- bring back (bring-brought-brought)

▲ a pyramid that the Maya built

## POP QUIZ

Who brought chocolate back to Europe?

ⓐ the Maya
ⓑ the Spanish

Much farther north, the Vikings raided settlements all over Europe.

Between the 8th and 11th centuries, the Vikings hunted, fought, fished, looted, and sailed.

Viking culture and mythology is still appreciated today.

Modern movies rely on tales of the Vikings.

Across the seas, the Maori sailed away from Polynesia in the 13th century.

Today, they still live, dance, and tattoo in New Zealand.

The Maori pass on their culture through many rituals.

One ritual is the haka, a Maori dance.

Rugby fans, especially, know the fierce haka.

▲ the Vikings

▲ the Maori

The Bedouins have roamed the deserts of Arabia since the 14th century.

▲ the Bedouins

In the harsh desert, people and animals stay on the move.
Bedouins offer hospitality to all who pass.
With tea, roasted lamb, spiced coffee, and music, Bedouins honor their guests.
Bedouin faith and hospitality live on today.

### KEY WORDS

- much
- farther
- raid
- settlement
- century
- fight (fight-fought-fought)
- loot
- sail
- mythology
- appreciate
- rely on

- tale
- Polynesia
- tattoo
- pass on
- ritual
- haka
- rugby
- fierce
- roam
- desert (cf. dessert)
- Arabia

- harsh
- on the move
- offer
- hospitality
- roasted
- spiced
- honor
- faith
- live on

# Chapter One

# In the Maya Jungle

The Maya civilization existed between 1,000 and 3,500 years ago. 🌐

Chac lived in a city in ancient Mexico that rose out of the jungle.

Chac was named for the god of rain and thunder.

His friend Nelli's name meant "truth."

The two friends liked to explore the jungle.

Chac's jungle was filled with monkeys, parrots, deer, and tree sloths.

Today, Chac and Nelli roamed the jungle and watched the birds.

There were hundreds of species of birds in the jungle.

Hummingbirds, hawks, and turkeys were among the birds.

**KEY WORDS**

- civilization
- exist
- rise (rise-rose-risen)
- name for
- thunder
- mean (mean-meant-meant)
- explore
- be filled with
- deer
- sloth
- hundreds of
- species
- hummingbird
- hawk
- turkey

There were also predators in the jungle.

Jaguars and pumas roamed freely.

The children didn't venture into the jungle alone at night.

Someday, Chac hoped to hunt jaguar like his father.

His father was known as a fierce warrior.

He wore jaguar teeth around his neck.

He wasn't the king, however.

Only the king wore a jaguar pelt.

**KEY WORDS**

- predator
- jaguar
- puma
- freely
- venture
- be known as (know-knew-known)
- warrior
- wear (wear-wore-worn)
- pelt
- pyramid
- temple

- tomb
- noble
- Egyptian
- step
- climb up
- track
- planet
- observatory
- circular
- opening
- observe

▲ Maya pyramid

▲ Maya observatory

The Maya built pyramids as temples and tombs for
nobles.

They were a similar shape to Egyptian pyramids.

Maya pyramids had many steps.

Chac and Nelli could climb up the outside of the
pyramids.

The Maya also made buildings to help track the planets,
the sun, and the stars.

These buildings, called observatories, were circular.

The walls had openings in them, like windows, to look
out and observe the stars.

The Maya kept information about the stars in books. The Maya believed the Earth was the center of the universe.
Unlike other ancient cultures, the Maya were able to predict eclipses.

▲ eclipse

By watching the moon and the sun, they noticed that sometimes one covered the other.

"Maybe I'll grow up to study the stars," Chac said.

"Instead of a hunter and warrior like your father?" Nelli asked.

"Yes," Chac answered.

**POP QUIZ**

What were the Maya able to do that other ancient cultures couldn't?

ⓐ make books
ⓑ predict eclipses

**KEY WORDS**

- keep (keep-kept-kept)
- information
- the universe
- unlike (↔ like)

- be able to + *Verb* (= can)
- predict
- eclipse
- notice

- sometimes
- maybe
- grow up (grow-grew-grown)
- instead of

Maya leaders made decisions based on the planets.

The cycles of Venus decided when the Maya went to war.

The heavens also determined what vegetables they planted and when.

▲ Maya calendar

The calendar system was also based on the movements in the sky. 🌐

The Maya calendar was one of the most accurate of the ancient world.

It was also one of the most complicated.

**KEY WORDS**

- **make a decision** (make-made-made)
- **based on**
- **cycle**
- **Venus**
- **decide**
- **go to war** (go-went-gone)

- the heavens
- determine
- calendar
- movement
- accurate
- complicated

"I can become a priest," Chac said.

"Then I'll get to work on the calendar."

Priests studied the sun, the moon, and the stars to note time passing.

The calendar had 18 months with 20 days and one month with five unlucky days.

Each month had a name and a picture.

Each day also had a name and a picture.

The pictures were called glyphs. 🌐

A glyph was a picture that represented a thing or a sound.

Glyphs took the forms of humans, animals, objects, and geometric and natural designs.

They were used to write words and sentences.

▲ glyphs

KEY WORDS

- priest
- work on
- note
- unlucky (↔ lucky)
- glyph

- represent
- take the form of (take-took-taken)
- object
- geometric

"As a priest, you'll get to write with glyphs," Nelli said.

"I'll teach you how, Nelli," Chac said.

"I can't wait," Nelli said.

They left the jungle and walked between a pyramid and the observatory.

"I'm thirsty," Nelli said.

"Let's go home and have some chocolate," Chac suggested.

At Chac's house, his mother poured liquid chocolate from one bowl held at waist level into another bowl on the ground.

Pouring back and forth from a distance made the drink become creamy and frothy.

Chocolate was the "drink of the gods."

The Maya didn't only drink chocolate.

They ate chocolate porridge and chocolate sauces.

"My mother usually prepares chocolate with corn meal, water, and honey," Nelli said.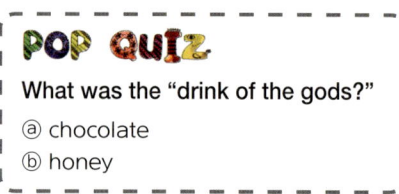

"My mother adds chili peppers," Chac said.

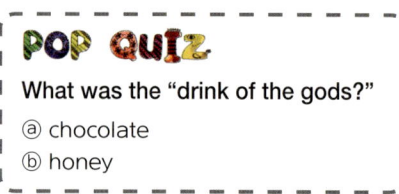

POP QUIZ

**What was the "drink of the gods?"**

ⓐ chocolate
ⓑ honey

**KEY WORDS**

- pour
- liquid
- hold (hold-held-held)
- waist
- back and forth

- from a distance
- creamy
- frothy
- porridge
- sauce

- usually
- prepare
- corn meal
- add
- chili pepper

Chocolate was used in wedding rituals, burials, and to honor gods and kings.

The Maya even used the cocoa beans as money.

Maya creation myths mention the cacao tree.

In one myth, a magical head hung on a cacao tree and became the father to twin gods.

In another myth, a god gave the cacao tree to the Maya.

Another myth tells how the gods discovered the cacao tree in a sacred place.

Chocolate was tied to the beginnings of the Maya, so it was very important to them.

▲ cocoa pods on a cacao tree

Chocolate played a role in religious ceremonies.
This may be why it was originally reserved for the elite.
When it was first eaten, it was too special for commoners.
However, by the time the Spanish arrived in the 1500s, everyone drank chocolate.
Chocolate was so important to the Maya, they had a goddess of chocolate!

**KEY WORDS**

- wedding
- burial
- even
- cocoa bean
- creation myth
- mention
- magical
- hang on (hang-hung-hung)
- sacred
- be tied to

- beginning
- play a role
- religious
- ceremony
- originally
- reserve
- the elite
- commoner
- by the time
- arrive

**A** Circle all the animals that Chac could see in the jungle.

deer

elephants

hamsters

lions

monkeys

parrots

polar bears

tree sloths

**B** Fill in each blank with the right word below.

goddess    pyramids    eclipses    king

❶ Only the _____ wore a jaguar pelt.

❷ The Maya built _____ as temples and tombs for nobles.

❸ The Maya were able to predict _____.

❹ The Maya had a _____ of chocolate.

**C** Choose the best answer to each question.

➊ Why did observatories have windows?

a) to get fresh air

b) to observe the stars

c) to guard the city

d) to watch birds in the jungle

➋ According to the story, what makes chocolate become creamy and frothy?

a) shaking the chocolate in a covered jar

b) adding milk to boiling chocolate

c) pouring it back and forth from a distance

d) stirring the chocolate

**D** Mark T for true or F for false.

➊ Maya pyramids had many steps on the outside.　　T　F

➋ The Maya believed the sun was the center of the universe.　　T　F

➌ Glyphs were used to take pictures of drawings.　　T　F

➍ The Maya used cocoa beans as money.　　T　F

# Chapter Two

# A Viking Village

The Vikings lived near the North Sea around 800 to 1150 AD.

The Vikings were from Norway, Sweden, and Denmark.

Their name means "pirate."

They sailed on ships to other countries to steal treasures.

When the Vikings weren't at war, they led simple lives.

**KEY WORDS**

- North Sea
- be from
- Norway
- Sweden
- Denmark

- pirate
- **steal** (steal-stole-stolen)
- treasure
- be at war
- **lead a simple life** (lead-led-led)

Helga lived in a stone house with thick walls.

Her long, rectangular house had rounded corners and a thatched roof.

Her name meant "holy or blessed."

She felt blessed to live with her large family in a warm home.

The fire was in the middle of their single room.

Everyone slept in the same room, near the fire and wrapped in furs.

The farm animals slept in the same room with Helga's family.

**KEY WORDS**

- rectangular
- rounded
- thatched roof
- holy
- blessed
- in the middle of
- wrap in
- furs

To Helga, home smelled of smoke and ash.

She usually wore a light linen dress, covered by a woolen outer dress. She and her mother spun flax into linen themselves.

▲ flax

The straps of her dress were held up by gilt oval brooches on Helga's shoulders.

She also wore a cap.

After a breakfast of bread and milk, Helga helped her mother around the house.

Her brothers harvested with their father.

Some days they went hunting.

"Helga, time to grind the corn," her mother called.

They walked to the mill with the other women of the village.

They put the grain on the millstones.

Each woman had to turn the mill, first in one direction, then the other.

It was tiring work.

Back at home, they used the flour to make flat bread.

They baked the bread in the embers of the fire.

Some women baked bread in a clay oven.

**POP QUIZ**

What did Helga bake in the embers of the fire?

ⓐ flat bread
ⓑ sweet cakes

**KEY WORDS**

- harvest
- go hunting
- grind
- mill
- grain
- millstone
- have to (have-had-had)
- direction

- the other
- tiring
- flour
- flat
- bake
- ember
- clay

"Please go collect eggs from the geese," Mother said in the afternoon.

On a normal day, the family ate the eggs with dinner.

They also dined on venison, walnuts, and elderberries.

Helga took a basket and walked through the yard.

Sometimes wild chickens wandered into the yard, too.

Back in the house, Mother was laying fruit near the fire.
Helga had picked the fruit yesterday.

"Come help me spread the rest of these berries for drying," Mother said.

Refrigerators didn't exist yet, so Vikings had to make the food last in other ways.

They preserved meat with salt or by smoking.

Dairy was made into cheese.

Fruit was dried by the fire.

Grains were made into bread and beer.

▲ elderberry

Tonight was one of the three Viking feast days.

This early spring feast was to ask the gods for victory in raids.

Helga's family would sacrifice a horse to the gods.

Such a sacrifice was meant to strengthen the gods.

In turn, the gods would grant favor on the people.

In addition to the eggs, venison, walnuts, and berries of a normal day, there would be other foods.

They would eat goat, pork, and the bread Mother and Helga baked earlier.

Her uncle, a fisherman, would bring fish.

She knew he often found whales washed up on the beach near their village.

He also went seal-hunting and salmon-fishing.

Her family also ate many other types of fish and seafood.

Her family ate fish fresh, salted, pickled, smoked, and dried.

These were the same methods they used to preserve meat.

Dessert was usually fresh fruit with honey and buttered bread.

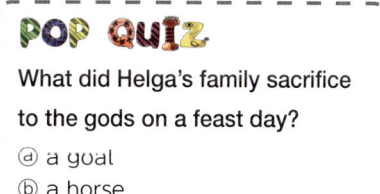

**POP QUIZ**

What did Helga's family sacrifice to the gods on a feast day?

ⓐ a goat
ⓑ a horse

Her oldest brother, Olaf, would set sail in a few days.

He and Father would take a longship to England. 🌐

In England, they hoped to join Eric Bloodaxe, a famous Viking leader.

He would later become a Viking king.

Someone would probably make a runestone about Eric Bloodaxe.

Runestones were big stones with words carved into them.

The words told about someone's life or about a great victory.

Eric Bloodaxe had many victories in England.

▲ rune          ▲ runestone

Sometimes they carved Thor's hammer into a runestone.

Thor was the most popular Viking god. 🌐

The god of thunder, Thor was very strong and carried a magic hammer.

Maybe they would make a runestone about Olaf's first journey across the North Sea.

Helga hoped Olaf and Father would be safe.

Raiding English towns could be dangerous.

▲ Thor

**POP QUIZ**

Who was Thor?

ⓐ the god of hammers
ⓑ the god of thunder

**KEY WORDS**

- oldest
- set sail (set-set-set)
- in a few days
- longship
- later
- probably

- runestone
- carved
- Thor
- hammer
- carry
- journey

Before dinner, Olaf polished his spear.

He was proud of his first weapon.

An iron blade topped a 2-meter-long wooden shaft.

He would be able to thrust it or throw it in battle.

Father had a long-handled battle axe.

It was too heavy for Helga to lift.  Aha!

"Why does Olaf get a spear while Father fights with a battle axe?" Helga asked.

"The spear is the most common weapon," Father answered.

"Someday Olaf might be able to afford a battle axe."

## POP QUIZ

**Match the two sides.**

ⓐ Olaf's weapon  •           •  ① was an axe.
ⓑ Father's weapon  •          •  ② was a spear.

### KEY WORDS

- polish
- spear
- be proud of
- weapon
- iron blade
- top
- wooden
- shaft

- thrust
- throw (throw-threw-thrown)
- battle
- long-handled
- axe
- while
- common
- afford

A few days later, Helga's family accompanied
Olaf and Father to the longship.

"Don't forget your shield," Helga called to Olaf.

His shield was a wooden circle covered with leather.

It had an iron hand grip in the middle.

Olaf had painted Thor's hammer on the rim.

In battle, Father wore a long tunic made of
interlocking metal rings called mail armor.
He also wore an iron helmet.
Olaf didn't have mail armor yet.
He would wear reindeer hide.
His cap was also made of hide.

**KEY WORDS**

- accompany
- forget
  (forget-forgot-forgotten)
- shield
- leather
- grip
- on the rim
- tunic
- made of
- interlock
- metal
- mail armor
- reindeer
- hide

On the longship, Olaf would sit on deck with the other men and row.

Viking ships were fast.

They used oars and sails.

"Father, what treasures will we find in England?" Olaf asked.

Father grunted. "Coins, gold, and silver, my son."

**KEY WORDS**

- deck
- row
- oar
- grunt
- load
- crate
- with tears in one's eyes

**42** • Chapter Two

Helga watched men lead horses onto the ship.

Father helped load crates of food.

Helga's mother kissed them goodbye with tears in her eyes.

"Come back safely," she said.

**POP QUIZ**

Why were Viking ships fast?

ⓐ They had a motor.

ⓑ They used oars and sails.

# Comprehension Quiz

**A** Choose all the words that describe Olaf's shield.

a) iron hand grip

b) made of bronze

c) covered with leather

d) made of iron

e) a painting of Thor's hammer on the rim

f) wooden circle

**B** Fill in each blank with the right word below.

| victory | furs | linen | hammer |
|---|---|---|---|

❶ Helga and her mother spun flax into _____ themselves.

❷ The early spring feast was to ask the gods for _____ in raids.

❸ Thor carried a magic _____.

❹ Everyone slept in the same room, near the fire and wrapped in

_____.

C  Choose the best answer to each question.

❶ Where was Helga's family's fire?

a) at one side of the long house

b) in the backyard of the house

c) in the heating room of the house

d) in the middle of their single room house

❷ Why did Helga's family sacrifice an animal?

a) because the animal was sick

b) for the meat

c) to sharpen the axe

d) to strengthen the gods

❸ What is the most common Viking weapon?

a) battle axe

b) hammer

c) spear

d) sword

# Chapter Three

# A Maori Feast

The Maori arrived in New Zealand from Polynesia in the 13th century.

They are still there today.

Rongo and his friend, Aata, liked to watch the warriors dance.

The Maori called their dances "haka."

Both men and women could perform haka.

They performed haka for many reasons.

They celebrated achievements.

They welcomed guests.

They performed a haka before a battle.

The men also danced in between hunting or fishing parties.

POP QUIZ

Mark T for true or F for false.

The Maori are no longer in New Zealand today.　　T / F

KEY WORDS

- both
- perform
- reason

- celebrate
- achievement
- party

Aata and Rongo practiced haka whenever they weren't busy working.

They hoped they would perform with the men when they were older.

The haka showed a tribe's pride and strength.

The men stomped their feet and chanted.

They slapped their bodies.

They stuck out their tongues.

It was a fierce dance.

In modern times, New Zealand's national rugby team is famous for its pre-game haka!

**POP QUIZ**

**What did the haka show?**

ⓐ a tribe's creative abilities
ⓑ a tribe's pride and strength

**KEY WORDS**

- whenever
- be busy + *Verb*-ing
- tribe
- pride
- strength
- stomp

- chant
- slap
- stick out (stick-stuck-stuck)
- national
- be famous for
- pre-game

"Look at me," Rongo told Aata.

He stuck out his tongue and stomped his feet.

Aata laughed.

"Now me," he said.

He slapped his thighs and stomped his feet.

Aata and Rongo loved to watch the young men dance.

They wanted to dance with them.

"Rongo, you must keep a good beat," Aata reminded him.

"Stand with confidence."

Rongo copied his friend's stance.

He stood with his feet apart and bent his knees.

"The footwork helps keep the beat," Rongo added.

They stomped just like the haka dancers.

"Move your hands to reflect the world," Aata said.

Their hands waved like the ocean.

They slapped their thighs.

"Now, reflect the rustling leaves," Rongo said.

They raised and lowered their hands.

When not dancing,
the boys helped their
families.
Everyone in the village
always worked together
at gardening, fishing,
hunting, and doing
chores.

▲ fern

Rongo's sister helped their mother with household
chores, like sweeping and preparing food.
She took care of their younger brothers and sisters.
Rongo helped by gathering roots and fruit, and
sometimes went hunting with the men.
Maori cultivated vegetable gardens and ate a lot of fern
root. (Aha!)
They also had barbecues.

Today, the men had dug a pit and built a fire in it.
Stones were left in the pit to heat up.
Later, they would cook meat,
potatoes, and yams in the pit.
It would take about three
hours.
Tonight, they would have a
feast.

▲ New Zealand yam

The men would dance a haka.
Tomorrow, everyone in the village would move north
before the arrival of winter.
They moved with the seasons for better hunting and
planting.
"Will you wear your whale pendant for the feast
tonight?" Aata asked Rongo.
Rongo nodded.
His father had given it to him.

**KEY WORDS**

- **dig** (dig-dug-dug)
- pit
- build a fire
- heat up
- yam
- arrival
- pendant

- firelight
- performance
- with wide eyes
- troupe
- once
- darkness

Later, after the feast, everyone danced and sang.

They played games.

Rongo's face shone in the firelight.

He and Aata watched the haka performance with wide eyes.

"Maybe they'll let us join the troupe when we're older," Rongo said.

Once the darkness came, they went to sleep.

The day ended early because it began early.

The next morning, Rongo and his family prayed to the
rising sun.

They did this every morning.

They raised their arms to the sun and sang.

Maori were also known for their tattoos, which they
called "moko." 🌐

Each moko design was unique.

It gave information about the person wearing the tattoo.

It told about their family, tribe, and accomplishments.

▲ moko

Moko were not just pretty to look at.
Moko were sacred to the Maori.
Moko was only performed by an expert in a sacred ritual.
Maori tattoos showed respect.
They also showed a person's commitment to Maori beliefs.
Unlike other tattoos, the skin wasn't punctured by needles.
Moko are carved into the skin by chisels.
So the skin wasn't left smooth.
Rongo's father's moko was on his face, chest and arms.
His mother had a swirly moko on her chin.

POP QUIZ
What are Maori tattoos called?
ⓐ haka
ⓑ moko

KEY WORDS

- pray
- be known for
- unique
- accomplishment
- expert

- show respect
- commitment
- belief
- puncture
- needle

- chisel
- smooth
- swirly
- chin

"My mother always tells the story of how moko came to be," Rongo said to Aata.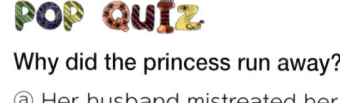

A young man fell in love with a princess of the underworld.

Her father was a moko expert.

At the time, moko was only known in the underworld.

Above ground, people only painted their faces.

They didn't chisel the designs.

The man and the princess married.

The man mistreated his wife one day and she ran away to the underworld.

The man followed her and overcame many obstacles.

---

## POP QUIZ

**Why did the princess run away?**

ⓐ Her husband mistreated her.
ⓑ She missed her father.

---

**KEY WORDS**

- **fall in love with** (fall-fell-fallen)
- **underworld**
- **marry**
- **mistreat**

- **run away** (run-ran-run)
- **follow**
- **overcome** (overcome-overcame-overcome)
- **obstacle**

When he reached his wife, his face paint had rubbed off.

He asked his father-in-law to teach him the art of moko.

He hoped learning moko would show his wife how sorry he was.

She forgave her husband.

When the husband and wife returned above ground, they brought the knowledge of moko with them.

"Oh Rongo, you like all the old stories," Aata said.

Rongo nodded.

"I love hearing about the gods and our ancestors."

Aata slapped Rongo's arm.

"Me, too, but right now I need to move and jump and dance. Let's practice haka."

**KEY WORDS**

- rub off
- father-in-law
- forgive (forgive-forgave-forgiven)
- knowledge
- ancestor
- right now

**A** Circle all the acts that Maori people did after the festival.

cooking                    playing games

dancing                    singing

hunting                    sweeping

**B** Fill in each blank with the right word(s) below.

| an expert | every morning | beliefs |
| --- | --- | --- |

❶ Rongo and his family prayed to the rising sun _____.

❷ Moko were sacred to the Maori. Moko was only performed by

_____.

❸ Maori tattoos showed a person's commitment to Maori

_____.

**C** Choose the best answer to each question.

**❶** Why is the footwork important in a haka?

a) It helps keep the beat.

b) It keeps the dancer from falling over.

c) It makes the dance fancy.

d) It makes the dance more difficult.

**❷** Why did the Maori move with the seasons?

a) for better hunting and planting

b) for a change of view

c) to go to war

d) to own more land

**❸** How are moko different from other tattoos?

a) Only moko are swirly.

b) The colors are different.

c) The skin isn't left smooth.

d) There aren't any words.

# Bedouin Hospitality

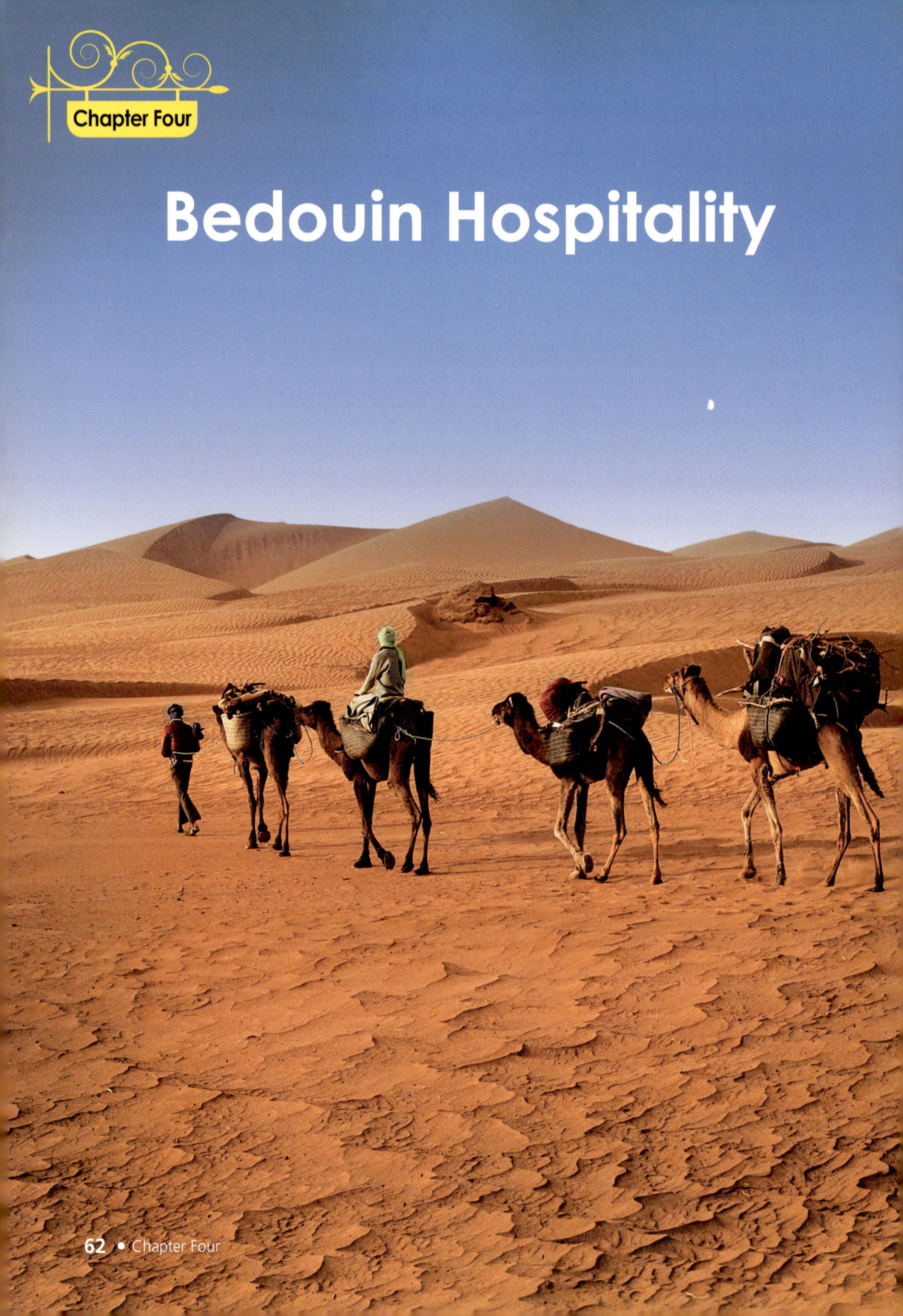

Bedouin tribes still travel throughout the deserts of the Middle East and North Africa. 🌐

They have been in these places since the 14th century.

Bedouin means "people who live in the desert."

Noora lived with her family in 1750.

Her name meant "light."

The desert is dry and hot, so Noora's family moved a lot.

They couldn't stay too long in one place.

No spot in the desert could support the life of a family for long.

There wasn't enough water or food.

They traveled the desert on foot and by camel.

They traveled from one oasis to another.

The vegetation of one oasis regrew while the family lived at another oasis.

Each oasis needed time to regrow.

They brought herds of goats and sheep with them.

**KEY WORDS**

- travel throughout
- Middle East
- North Africa
- spot
- support
- enough

- camel
- oasis
- vegetation
- regrow (regrow-regrew-regrown)
- herd

The desert was so big and so quiet, that they didn't meet people often.

When they did, it was a special event.

So Noora's family treated visitors very well.

Visitors became almost part of the family.

The family protected them even during wars.

Today, a stranger appeared outside Noora's tent.

Her family's tent was made of camel hair. Other Bedouin tents could be made of goat hair. It was divided into two spaces by a curtain. One side was for the men and male guests. The other was for the women. It was where they cooked and welcomed female guests.

"Noora," her father called. "We have a guest."

**POP QUIZ**

What was Noora's family's tent made of?
ⓐ camel hair
ⓑ horse hair

**KEY WORDS**

- treat
- protect
- during
- stranger

- appear
- tent
- be divided into
- space

- curtain
- male (*cf.* female)

Like other Bedouin men, the guest wore a long robe.
On his head, he wore a cloth and a rope around his
forehead.

This rope demonstrated a man's status.

Noora's father and brothers wore the same cloth and
rope combination.

To welcome the guest, Noora and her sisters spread out
a rug.

The guest entered the tent and Noora served him sweet
tea.

Sweet tea was the first part of the ritual for welcoming
guests.

Noora's family ate whatever meat traveled with them. They cooked goat and sheep over a fire or in underground ovens.

Noora's brothers would dig a hole in the sand about a meter deep.

They lined the sides with bricks.

They'd lay strips of lamb in the oven. 📖 Aha!

Then, they'd cover the top with sand mixed with water or with bricks.

It could take all day to cook.

---

**POP QUIZ**

How did Noora's family cook goats and sheep?

ⓐ in underground ovens
ⓑ over bricks

---

**KEY WORDS**

- robe
- cloth
- demonstrate
- status
- combination
- spread out

- rug
- serve
- whatever
- underground
- line
- strip

Bedouins couldn't carry many fresh vegetables or fruit.

Dates were often available and dried easily.

Goats, camels, and sheep also produced milk.

Noora's family made yogurt and butter with the milk.

Bedouins dried yogurt to preserve it, just like fruit.

Noora's mother made fresh bread every day.

She made lots of different types of bread.

Some baked in the underground oven.

Some baked on a stone tray on a fire.

After dinner, the women prepared for the next part of the ritual for guests.

"Now for the coffee," her mother said, on the women's side of the tent.

▲ date

The women's hair was covered and they wore long, bright dresses. Mother wore a black cloth wrapped around her head. When they left the tent, the women wore an embroidered black coat. Women kept their hair covered as a matter of respect.

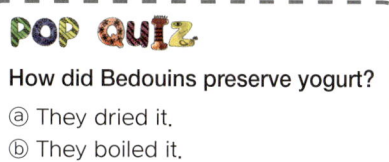

Noora's mother roasted coffee beans.

Then, she ground them in a mortar.

Noora mixed the ground coffee with cardamom pods and water in a pot.

The pot was brass with a long beak.

Noora boiled the coffee three times to make it strong.

▲ cardamom pod

**POP QUIZ**

How did Bedouins preserve yogurt?

ⓐ They dried it.
ⓑ They boiled it.

Noora lifted the platter to carry it through the curtain.

"Noora, wait!" Mother said.

"The cloth has slipped off your head."

She pulled the platter from Noora's arms so she could fix the cloth.

Only Father and Noora's brothers were allowed to see the girls without hair coverings.

Once she was presentable again, Noora brought the coffee to the men's side of the tent.

They served the spiced coffee in tiny china cups.

"What lovely egg-shaped cups," the guest said. Aha!

They only filled the cups halfway.

"Thank you, Noora," Father said.

He drank the first cup to show the guest the coffee was safe.

Then they served the guest as much coffee as he wanted.

**KEY WORDS**

- platter
- slip off
- be allowed to + *Verb*
- without
- covering
- presentable
- china cup
- lovely
- egg-shaped
- halfway

Noora's family entertained the guest with poetry, song, dance, and music.

Father played a flute made out of a metal pipe.

The eldest brother, Ibrahim, played a sort of violin with only one string.

It was called a "rababa."

Noora and her sisters sang songs of praise.

**KEY WORDS**

- entertain
- poetry
- play

- flute
- made out of
- pipe

- eldest
- a sort of
- praise

Hospitality wasn't the only result of the harsh desert.

To survive, Bedouins worked together.

They had a strong sense of community.

Even children Noora's age helped.

The family couldn't survive the difficult conditions

unless everyone did his or her part.

**KEY WORDS**

- result
- survive
- a sense of community
- condition
- unless

The Bedouin followed many rules.

They prayed every day.

Prayer required ritual washing.

They washed with water if they had any.

Otherwise, they washed with sand.

A Bedouin always greeted each person he met or welcomed into the tent.

When welcoming a group, he started with the person on the right and continued in a counter-clockwise direction.

It was the same for meals.

They served the person to the right first and then continued counter-clockwise.

**POP QUIZ**

When there was no water, what did Bedouins use to wash their hands?

ⓐ alcohol

ⓑ sand

**KEY WORDS**

- require
- washing
- otherwise
- greet
- continue
- counter-clockwise
- have to do with
- grave

- loved one
- in need
- pass by
- in need of
- provide
- shelter
- truly

Another rule of Noora's people had to do with clothing.
When a Bedouin died, his family left his clothes on top
of his simple grave.

In this way, the dead loved one could help anyone in
need who passed by.

"How do the clothes help travelers?" Noora asked her
mother.

"Travelers in the desert are often in need of something,"
she answered.

All Bedouins were happy to provide clothing, food, or
shelter.

It honored God for Bedouins to honor their guests.

They believed God would in turn be good to them.

Hospitality was truly important to the Bedouins.

# Comprehension Quiz

**A** Choose the best answer to each question.

❶ Why did Noora's family travel constantly?

a) They have family in faraway places.

b) They liked to wander.

c) There wasn't enough water or food.

d) They were running away.

❷ What was the first part of the ritual for welcoming guests?

a) coffee

b) dancing

c) music

d) sweet tea

**B** Put the sentences in order.

❶ Noora boiled the coffee three times to make it strong.

❷ Noora's mother ground coffee beans in a mortar.

❸ Noora's mother roasted coffee beans.

❹ Noora mixed the ground coffee with cardamom pods and water in a pot.

_____ → _____ → _____ → _____

C Solve the crossword puzzle.

❷ Where the vegetation grows in a desert?

❺ This is the spice put in the coffee made for guests.

❻ Where do the Bedouins live?

❶ Bedouins believe God wants them to _____ guests.

❸ This is an animal Noora's family traveled with.

❹ This is a food made from milk that the Bedouins dried.

❺ What did the Bedouins leave on top of the graves of loved ones?

# Let's Review the Story

Fill in the blanks to review the story.

**Title**: Amazing _____ of the World

**Place**: Mexico, _____ Europe, New Zealand, M _____

## Chapter 1: The Maya
- The Maya are from ancient M _____ .
- Their c _____ is complicated and accurate.
- They drank a lot of _____ .

## Chapter 2: The Vikings
- The Vikings lived near the N _____ Sea.
- They sailed on _____ .
- They left behind stories on r _____ .

## Chapter 3: The Maori
- The Maori live in _____ .
- They are known for their fierce d _____ .
- Their _____ were sacred to them.

## Chapter 4: The Bedouins
- The Bedouins are from the _____ of the Middle East and North Africa.
- They t _____ from oasis to oasis.
- They treat g _____ very well.

# Let's Think & Talk

Think about the following questions and answer them freely.

❶ Which of the four cultures in this book would you want to experience if you could go to an ancient time? Tell us why you chose that ethnic group's culture.

❷ There are many ethnic groups that have various and unique cultures around the world. Find out about the different UNESCO World Heritages there are, organize them, and tell us which one draws your attention the most.

❸ Knowing other countries and other ethnic groups' cultures is important, but knowing our own culture is also important. Check out what special cultural heritages you have and tell your friends about them.

# Let's Review the Story

**Title**: Amazing [ Ancient Cultures ] of the World

**Place**: Mexico, [ Northern ] Europe, New Zealand, [ Middle East ]

## Chapter 1: The Maya
- The Maya are from ancient [ Mexico ].
- Their [ calendar ] is complicated and accurate.
- They drank a lot of [ chocolate ].

## Chapter 2: The Vikings
- The Vikings lived near the [ North ] Sea.
- They sailed on [ longships ].
- They left behind stories on [ runestones ].

## Chapter 3: The Maori
- The Maori live in [ New Zealand ].
- They are known for their fierce [ dances ].
- Their [ tattoos ] were sacred to them.

## Chapter 4: The Bedouins
- The Bedouins are from the [ deserts ] of the Middle East and North Africa.
- They [ travel ] from oasis to oasis.
- They treat [ guests ] very well.

Smart Readers: **Wise** & **Wide**

# After-reading Test

- Amazing Ancient Cultures of the World
- Level 4
- 27 Questions

(Vocabulary 7 / Reading Comprehension 16 /

Sentence Structure & Grammar 4)

1. What is a "desert"?
   ① a place that is dry and hot
   ② a place that is hot and misty
   ③ another name for a war
   ④ something you eat at the end of a meal

2. Which of the following is the wrong past tense form of the verb?
   ① spun                    ② laid
   ③ regrow                  ④ stuck

3. Which of the following is NOT a word about shapes?
   ① oval                    ② circular
   ③ rectangular             ④ underground

※ Choose the right word for each blank. (4~5)

4.
   The jungle was filled _____ monkeys, parrots, deer, and tree sloths.

   ① like                    ② with
   ③ to                      ④ off

5.
   She took care _____ their younger brothers and sisters.

   ① of                      ② into
   ③ at                      ④ towards

6. What is the common word for the two blanks?

> • Modern movies rely _____ tales of the Vikings.
> • The Maori pass _____ their culture through many rituals.

① on                                    ② for

③ to                                    ④ with

7. What are the proper words for the blanks?

> • Chocolate _____ a role in religious ceremonies.
> • Today, the men had dug a pit and _____ a fire in it.
> • A young man _____ in love with a princess of the underworld.

① took — played — made

② tasted — built — stopped

③ played — boiled — fell

④ played — built — fell

※ Choose the right answer to each question about the Maya. (8~11)

8. When did the Maya civilization exist?

　① 500 years ago

　② between 750 and 900 years ago

　③ between 1,000 and 3,500 years ago

　④ 4,000 years ago

9. Who wore jaguar teeth around their neck?

　① children                          ② gods

　③ servants                          ④ warriors

10. What shape were Maya observatories?
    ① rectangular        ② circular
    ③ triangle        ④ square

11. What could take the form of humans, animals, objects, and geometric and natural designs?
    ① calendars        ② glyphs
    ③ jaguars        ④ pyramids

※ Choose the right answer to each question about the Vikings. (12~15)

12. When did the Vikings live?
    ① 100 ~ 300 BC
    ② 100 ~ 500 AD
    ③ around 800 to 1150 AD
    ④ 1500 ~ 2000 AD

13. How did Helga hold up the straps of her dress?
    ① with gilt brooches
    ② with metal snaps
    ③ with wooden buttons
    ④ with zippers

14. How did the Vikings reach England?
    ① by airplane
    ② by horse
    ③ by longship
    ④ by swimming

15. Why did the Vikings make runestones?
    ① to mark off a garden
    ② for protection around a village
    ③ to tell about a great victory
    ④ to write messages to their family

※ Choose the right answer to each question about the Maori. (16~19)
16. When did the Maori arrive in New Zealand from Polynesia?
    ① in the 3rd century
    ② in the 10th century
    ③ in the 13th century
    ④ in the 20th century

17. What are haka?
    ① children                    ② dances
    ③ gods                        ④ tattoos

18. Where did the Maori cook meat, potatoes, and yams?
    ① in the pit
    ② on a stove
    ③ in the sand
    ④ in a wood-fired oven

19. Why was each moko design unique?
    ① Each design is on a different part of the body.
    ② Each design is made for a different god.
    ③ It gave information about the moko artist.
    ④ It gave information about the person wearing the tattoo.

※ Choose the right answer to each question about the Bedouins. (20~23)

20. Bedouin tribes traveled throughout what part of the world?
    ① Ancient Mexico
    ② the Middle East
    ③ Polynesia
    ④ Southern Africa

21. How did Noora's family treat visitors?
    ① like enemies
    ② like part of the family
    ③ like strangers
    ④ very poorly

22. What did Noora's family make with the milk?
    ① bread and beer
    ② cheese
    ③ ice cream
    ④ yogurt and butter

23. What did Noora's mother wear around her head?
    ① an embroidered headband
    ② a black cloth
    ③ a brightly-colored cloth
    ④ a tall hat

※ Choose the wrong part of each sentence. (24~26)

24.
Aata and Rongo <u>practiced</u> haka <u>whenever</u> they <u>weren't</u> busy <u>work</u>.
                     ①                ②           ③       ④

25.
They loved <u>to watch</u> <u>the</u> young <u>men</u> <u>danced</u>.
         ①    ②          ③   ④

26.
My mother <u>prepares</u> <u>usually</u> chocolate <u>with</u> corn meal,
             ①               ②     ③

water, <u>and</u> honey.
     ④

27. Choose the correct sentence.
   ① My mother tells always the story how does moko come to be.
   ② My mother tells always the story of how did moke come to be.
   ③ My mother always tells the story on how came moko be to.
   ④ My mother always tells the story of how moko came to be.

**Brooke Rousseau**

Brooke Rousseau is a writer, mother, and French teacher who strives to make the exotic familiar. Driven by a fascination with other cultures, Brooke has lived in Europe, Africa, and the United States, and visited parts of the Middle East and South America. She has earned degrees in French Literature and International Relations. Brooke writes nonfiction for older elementary children, short stories for very young children, and middle grade and young adult novels.

 Smart Readers
Wise & Wide 4-4

# Amazing Ancient Cultures of the World

Written by Brooke Rousseau
Illustrated by Sohyeon Lee

First Published in July 2015

Editorial Manager: Juyon Choi
Editors: Kyunghee Jang, Jiyeong Park
Designers: Eunhee Lee, Elim
Cover Designer: Eunhee Lee

Published and distributed by

 Happy House

Darakwon Bldg., 64-1 Jandari-ro, Mapo-gu, Seoul, Korea 121-894
Tel: 82-2-736-2031(ext. 250)     Fax: 82-2-732-2037
Homepage: www.ihappyhouse.co.kr
Publisher: Kyudo Chung

ISBN: 978-89-6653-200-1 18740 / 978-89-6653-156-1 18740(set)

[Components]
• 1 Audio CD (Recording Studio: Aram)
• Answer Keys & Korean Translation: Free download at www.ihappyhouse.co.kr